CONQUEST

Zoë Brigley was born in 1981 and grew up in Caerphilly in the Rhymney Valley. She won an Eric Gregory Award in 2003 and received an Academi bursary in 2005. Her first book of poems, *The Secret* (Bloodaxe Books, 2007), was a Poetry Book Society Recommendation, and was long-listed for the Dylan Thomas Prize in 2008. Her second collection, *Conquest* (Bloodaxe Books, 2012), is also a Poetry Book Society Recommendation.

She is the co-editor of a volume of scholarly essays, *Feminism, Literature and Rape Narratives* (Routledge, 2010), and a collection of women's poetry, *Bluebeard's Wives* (Heaventree, 2007). She has taught creative writing at Warwick University and at University of Northampton, where she is a Research Fellow, and is currently living in Pennsylvania, USA.

ZOË BRIGLEY

CONQUEST

BLOODAXE BOOKS

Poems copyright © Zoë Brigley 2012
Artwork © Victoria Brookland 2012

ISBN: 978 1 85224 930 4

First published 2012 by
Bloodaxe Books Ltd,
Highgreen,
Tarset,
Northumberland NE48 1RP.

www.bloodaxebooks.com
For further information about Bloodaxe titles
please visit our website or write to
the above address for a catalogue.

Supported by
ARTS COUNCIL
ENGLAND

Cover design: Neil Astley & Pamela Robertson-Pearce.

Printed in Great Britain by
Bell & Bain Limited, Glasgow, Scotland.

*For my mother and grandmothers
simply for being the women they are.*

I had a feeling that Pandora's box contained the mysteries of woman's sensuality, so different from a man's and for which man's language was so inadequate. The language of sex had yet to be invented. The language of the senses was yet to be explored.

ANAÏS NIN, *The Delta of Venus*

CONTENTS

THE LADY AND THE UNICORN
A sequence after the tapestries at Musée de Cluny, Paris

MY LAST ROCHESTER

He scraped through the dark sand to the center house, two stories, both pouring bands of light into the fog. There was warmth and gaiety within, through the downstairs window he could see young people gathered around a piano, their singing mocking the forces abroad on this cruel night. She was there, protected by happiness and song and the good. He was separated from her only by a sand yard and a dark fence, by a lighted window and by her protectors.

DOROTHY B. HUGHES, *In a Lonely Place*

My Last Rochester

She's in the attic room in a Georgian house
in the town that you knew but never liked.
She waits for a bridegroom to arrive home
when he will play the double bass
stretching the gentle bow across the strings
as rain gathers in islands on the slanted windows.

What did you wear, that last time she saw you?
The moleskin coat bought together.
In her dreams, it flaps its ravenous wings
beside the bead of your empty crow eye.
She's writing after so long, sensible or not.
She's not asking for anything, not ever.

You're probably on your way somewhere,
about to catch a bus or a train, smelling of soap
and holding a tattered rucksack. Or maybe
you're only boiling roots in the kitchen,
imagining the saucepan as a big top
silver-lidded over the performers.

She remembers how sitting on the beaten-up sofa,
you said, 'I'll have you for my own',
and she believed you. Or there was the time
off Taksim Square when you last punched her,
your fist in her stomach, and afterwards,
you both made your way to the hotel in silence.

She hadn't thought of you for a while
until a friend of yours called and told her this:
that you were travelling again, Paris or Naples,
that you had found someone else
and this other woman was at last
the second person in your life that you'd loved.

And she wanted to ask if the first person was her
or if it ever figured at all? Her last Rochester,
I wanted to tell you that there isn't a day
that goes by that she doesn't think of you,
and yet for all that, it was never you at all.
It was never you that she wanted.

Behind the Looking Glass

She tries not to remember the things he did to her,
never a sound, so she is watching behind glass.
Her cheek presses against the pane, her breath
fogging the window, while something scrambles
outside in the dingy yard; the light switch
twitches on. Certain things do come back to her.
How on the way home from the pub, her legs
collapsed beneath her. How she was so light
that he carried her home, not for love's sake,
but to turn her over and over in his hands.
How whenever he left her, he would kiss
her forehead while she pretended to sleep,
and he pretended not to notice. How sometimes
he held her, his fingers making long strokes
along her golden head. How she wandered
the yard without eating, pulling her sleeves down
over her wrists where he'd hurt her.
How she realised at last that not even love
could justify this, that no affection could, not ever.
Still, in the glass, she sees her own mouth,
opening and closing and silent as a fish.

The Bell Confessing

At the Brontë Parsonage Museum in Yorkshire

Alone in the archive, I handle their belongings:
a tiny book written in meticulous script;
the hair bracelet; a snuff box from Brussels;
the perfume that belonged to their mother.
When the church-bells toll, they are up there
in the tower: their mouths opening to speak
while the audience gasps with hands full
of rope, and the taste of honeyed candlewax.

Up on the slate roof, a nest of pigeons
is murmuring never-told secrets.
I recall my own riddles: the unspoken truth
of you and I, our silent closeness that is for me
a sweet, blank victory. But in midnight dreams,
they confess a word with every bell-toll
and beg me to recount it all –
to tell their stories, my story, and I do.

Hair Bracelet

After it was plaited so that each tiny thread
wound this way and that to bind the band
together, I took my bangle of tawny hair
to the jewellers, where the elaborate weave
of the hair bracelet was fitted with a golden clasp
and a stone, the colour of yew berries.
Nothing could match the twine
of my golden armlet, except perhaps
after I died, when the severed curls
of my sisters and I wound their way
to each other in their funeral envelopes.

The Dispensary

In the dispensary of the Brontës' doctor
and with our marriage still a year away,
I think of the first time that we came here,
walking the steepness of Haworth,
the hill: climbing but never quite
reaching the Withens. From the bed
in the small hotel room, my gaze passes
through the window to float over Haworth:
the sheer mill chimney, the stark whiteness
of a wind turbine that tenses its blades
against the gale. Walking the cobbles to town,
I recall a morning outside Haworth Church
when the trees, which never existed
in the Brontës' time, made an aisle
for me to walk, and the leaves trembled
with the whisper of a promise and I felt them
like the hands of a very first lover.

The Scent Bottle

the vessel in which she had sent my box, being stranded on the coast
of Devonshire, in consequence of which the box was dashed to pieces
with the violence of the sea & all my little property, with the exception
of a very few articles, swallowed up in the mighty deep

MARIA BRANWELL, mother of the Brontë sisters,
in a letter to her future husband, Patrick Brontë

It is a long time coming but when it does arrive,
it sits by the mirror, the glass body protruding
a severed stalk, silver eye, squat key.

I sit before it as if waiting for something
and cradle the shock of its cold body in my palm.
It is not as beautiful as when it was new

– blasted by salt and scratched by sailors –
and yet, in the deep heady scent of it
is something else: an ocean voyage skimming

the North Sea and rounding the coast for Penzance
to the blink of a teasing lighthouse,
the long beckoning of a weathered stone pier,

the slap of pilchards on the cobbles, and coracles
dwarfed by larger vessels: the *Amity* and *Fame*,
the *Grace*, the *One and All* and the *Happy Return*.

In its perfume is not only a wilderness of roses,
but the watery stench of the tide-waiter and mariner,
the pasteboard smell of printers and bookbinders,

the sickly maltsters on Market Jew Street
and the burnt liquorice of the tanners and saddlers,
the tang of the physician's, the caramel of boot-makers,

the foggy wool of the tailors and drapers,
the peruke maker's flowery chamber
and honeyed fat of the tallow-chandler,

grasping soot in the deepening shaft of Wherry Mine
and smelted tin, rasping metallic blood on the tongue,
until the cork fits it again and that other place sets sail.

We wait together, the bottle and I, in the garden
where a patchwork moor spreads out before us
as a rough and mothering ocean and I stumble

out into the heather catching another scent on the wind.

NOTE: *tide-waiter:* customs official; *maltster:* maker of malt; *peruke maker:* wig maker;
tallow-chandler: a maker of candles from the suet or fat of animals.

Night-sea Journey

I must somehow have fallen over-board, or... there must have been a wreck at last. I too well remember a time – a long time, of cold, of danger, of contention.

CHARLOTTE BRONTË, *Villette*

From pier or rock I thought I knew the sea
– the taut delight in rough and briny waves –
and waited there eager for a midnight journey.

I find myself still lulling one idea,
but should have known under my childhood eaves,
from pier and rock, you cannot know the sea.

Rocked at midnight, all the listeners hear
the tempest gorge its pressure; offshore it raves,
greedy and eager on its ocean journey.

The broken hull is shattered by degrees;
the night-lamp of my lungs can find no ease,
but sets alight the waters of the sea.

When morning comes, the crows are sound asleep;
their wings drop pitch-black plumes for the bereaved:
a thousand weepers pray on their journeys.

And younger women – basking, happy, plump –
now long for salt of saint-devouring storms.
From pier or rock, they think they know the sea
and wait there hoping for a night-sea journey.

Passage

In the beginning, she was a passenger
and the first man she knew was a storm
that stopped her voyage dead in unknown waters.
Later, she was the captain issuing feeble orders
and going down bravely with the ship,
crushed under the weight of water and iron.

The crew could not believe it: a tempest so bloody,
and watermen who bid for her would only stir
a darkness they could not satisfy. She recalled
offering herself to delight or danger, and how
a hurricane shook her by the throat and lips.
She blamed herself, reproached her rashness.

She pictured herself as lightning, or as an empty sky
with neither sun nor moon. Every night in dreams,
the storm put its hands on her and her distress
pealed out of her as thunder. She dressed herself,
and split, and dressed again; she braved the ocean,
and armoured once more while all the crew perished.

And the storm laid her alight in agony,
a red monsoon: too terrible, glorious, royal.
He carried her over land and ocean; he crushed
her in wrecks, became a destroying angel in a single day.
She recalled very well what could excite her,
too well remembered the water-clogged boat.

Now, she sits on the quayside with the basking fishwives;
they watch the ladies go by with the protection of cloisters,
those women who are never to sail out of harbour.
Now she sees them pass and knows she is at equinox;
balancing the sun and moon, grief and hope,
she flies like a wild goose over the ocean.

Diptych for a Pear Tree

I *The Nun in the Pear Tree Bower*

On a quest to find you, after journeys by sea,
sickened by waves and cursed by sailors,
I find myself a nun in a silent oratory
wishing for speech in a low and gloomy room
lit by a crucifix and the vigil of two candles.

A child, I sleep in my narrow bed, as the stove
spits chips and fills the room with smoke.
Beyond my lattice grille, the thud of branches
on the window: a broken pear tree
calls me to haunt the startled orchard.

The purple anthers of pear tree blossom,
stiffen with fright; flowers fall away to snow
revealing the brown-rot of blackened branches.
One pear tree above others is my own Methuselah
– a granite slab at its roots hides a crypt.

Deep and leafy in my seclusion,
I wait for the fruiting of my giant pear tree,
the honey of its pendulous fruit.
Now for the stripping of my narrow skirt:
the becoming skeleton of my nunning pear tree.

Unwind my bandage, my chalked veil,
as the tongue finds carpel, seed and pip,
and at the heart of the pear, your eye
reveals itself to have known of my coming,
to have watched me all along.

Ah Monsieur! I once wrote you a letter which was hardly rational,
because sadness was wringing my heart, but I shall do so no more.

CHARLOTTE BRONTË in a letter to Constantin Heger

It was the note that you were expecting
when I said goodbye last time. I longed
to be your mistress, but never expected it
– just the opposite. My letter to you bloomed
to a flowering pear tree, the stamen soaked
with dew as my heart rustled. I couldn't sleep,
but instead cracked open the night with all
the feelings I had for you, the letter I was writing.

The words swollen in me, the syrupy ink
dropping from wet blossoms as purple elixir.
Somehow you knew my feelings before I did:
the slow fruiting of a pendulous pear
that we brewed to ripening wine together.
I lay under the pear tree all night to wait
– you could have kissed me – but there was
nothing but *bitterzoet* and the ghost
of the tree: the thumping of my buried heart.

In the roots of the giant pear tree, I put away
my letter, and now the weeds grow over it.
Mouldering pages fold round themselves at the root:
their hiding place. The spaces between words
are summer storms – love grows out of them.
But my aged pear-tree becomes a conductor:
crippled by lightning, it withers to fruit no more,
and I count passing years in letters you never sent.

Diptych after Anne Brontë

I *Anne of the Opening Hand*

In the overgrown garden, the winter days pass
as the long black column of a funeral train:
the hands of the mourners sheathed in white gloves,
their blank fingers pale and missing the nail.

Beside the blighted Scotch firs, the boxwood swan,
and the castellated towers of the bleeding laurels,
he considers the risk of encounter, whether
it is safer to admire me from this distance.

Out there in the wilderness, his hands strike
poses: trees and shrubs under a gardener's shears.
They readily assume the shapes I give them:
the swallow and warrior, the lion or goblin.

He reaches the garden gate never saying a word,
though the branches on the window sound
a round of applause. All that is left
is a hand waning, reaching across this parting hour.

II *Landlocked*

*Were an alteration to take place while she was far from home and alone
with you – it would be too terrible – the idea of it distresses me inextricably,
and I tremble whenever she alludes to the project of a journey. In short
I wish we could gain time and see how she gets on*

CHARLOTTE BRONTË in a letter about her sister Anne's
proposed trip to Scarborough

During the long night, Anne writes her desires:
a goodbye letter that sketches a glass-flat sea.

But I cannot bear her to leave and by morning,
I have soaked her letter with words of my own.

She rises at dawn and chalks the streets with pledges
to walk the narrow edge of cliff-top verges.

I stand below her window and above she listens
for donkey carts that rumble on a faraway beach.

She drinks the bland nectar of dandelion tea
with oranges ripe enough to eat on the sand.

She fills up the silence with a long caress
that makes little impression on my firm footing.

Still the water rises, the gulf will fill:
she floats like a boat out of landlock.

The Mourner

I've lived the parting hour to see

CHARLOTTE BRONTË, 'On the Death of Anne Brontë'

On Scarborough beach,
I stand on the sand and crows
fly out of my dress.

For long years, instead
of a heart, I've had a red eye
that watches and scries.

Somewhere is a house
with an ocean view: a crone
that sits on the porch.

I sit on the stoop
by the sea and my stockings
and dress are all black.

But even now, love
grows: an anemone tongue
in her mouth, my mouth.

Under my skirt, she's
beating her wings, breaking me
apart, setting me free.

Daughter

Something is stirring in the old wheelhouse
where I listen at night under mutters of snow:
the moan of salted wood against crippling waves,
and the rock and ebb of a cradling crib.

A train at the end of the line is turned,
its pistons silent, braced for revolutions.
Between the ancient stones of the wheelhouse barrow
darkness is nesting, stubborn as cement or clay.

Something black is crossing the hillside snow:
a dark orb on the white wing of a butterfly,
a beaded owl eye nesting in creamy feathers,
a black beetle hunting on the face of a clock.

In the wheelhouse of the dark, my ghost daughter
stirs, enters my heart through black and briny blood
that beats in spasms. She's inside me somewhere
in a place I can't reach, like seabeds where no sound has been.

The Fir Tree Prisoner

I heard distinctly the gusty wind, and the driving of the snow; I heard, also, the fir bough repeat its teasing sound.

EMILY BRONTË, *Wuthering Heights*

In my night dreams, a fir-tree hand knocks
its knuckle on the windowpane. Try as I might,
I cannot force the glass out of its soldered frame,
but the fir remains my night companion,
stiffening in its bark at sunrise, and when I wake
the bedclothes are soaked by dew, or milk, or sap.

The Tin Soldier

The little maid was stretching out both arms, for she was a dancer, and
in the dance, one of her legs was raised so high into the air that the
tin soldier could see absolutely nothing of it, and he supposed that she,
like himself, had but one leg.

HANS CHRISTIAN ANDERSEN, 'The Steadfast Tin Soldier'

On the night of our marriage, I press
my cold forehead against the bridegroom's cheek
as we look out the window over golden town spires
that glow under sunset like a dream of promise.

Looking into the fall of darkness is gazing
into a shroud: a woman veiled white for a bride
and black in the Spanish lace of a mourner,
with a face underneath of plaster and porcelain.

Lately I find that my head will not fit the pillow
when I lie in bed at my bridegroom's side,
because the room is small and flickers by candlelight
and the air is thick with the taste of molten metal.

I still remember the stories of my childhood
and if I am the ballerina, fashioned in paper,
self-consuming by flame, then he must be the tin soldier,
fighting flood, fear, appetite, to carry home his white-hot heart.

The Plum Tree Suicide

How happy I was at the gift of a midnight plum,
my very first taste sucked to a stone, its juice
glistening on parched lips that hungered all night
with dreams of orchards rustling in the dark.
How wretched I was by fall when the foetus-bulbs
of purpling fruit fell from the branches to rot.
What I would have given for even one plum, when
under the branches, my slit veins darkened the soil.
How surprised I am that I'm still alive –
it was the plum tree that died, not me withering.
I am somewhere else, eating apples, oranges, pears,
anything to take this taste from my mouth.

The Spinner

The jack-in-the-box has a smiling face
and ratchets its spring through the blackout.
Even in sleep, we await the jolt:
the horror and cramp of its presence.

What little we have brings us pleasure: the ripening
damask drapes, a fraying armchair sheathed
in voile, the fireplace roasting the tiles
as the coals whiten and fall into ash.

Everything in the room cushions our desire,
though his lips are always at the keyhole
as if whispering there could be an entrance
or muster the grace of a long-ago key.

He finds his way under the stark alley lamp,
while I watch the door from an old tin bath.
I turn all night on a gilded box,
and spin myself to paper, to fire, to clay.

The Adventuress

Sometimes I find myself spirited away
as I wait in woods for my bridegroom.
All that is left of me is a silver locket,
that hangs on a branch at the heart of winter.

Waiting for my bridegroom in frosted woods,
I find myself bound in a breathless crinoline.
Hung in the trunk, my winter heart
is corseted by the snow-laden oak.

The trees are bound and up-ended crinolines,
as they wade through drifts and foggy sleep.
The snow-laden oak struggles in its corset
so twigs and brushwood collapse to snow-beds.

Fighting the drifts and foggy sleep,
in snow thigh-deep, I dig for my bridegroom.
My lace collar and petticoat collapse to snowflakes
as I reach his shoulder frozen by blizzards.

Journeying towards him, I am the secret of the woods
as my silks fall away to a silver locket.
Beneath my dress is a ladder of desire,
that I climb tonight and each night after that.

CONQUEST

Controlling women's sexuality, exalting maternity and breed-
ing a virile race of empire-builders were widely perceived as
the paramount means for controlling the health and wealth
of the male imperial body politic, so that... sexual purity
emerged as the controlling metaphor for racial, economic
and political power.'

ANNE McCLINTOCK, *Imperial Leather*

Glyph

Millions are condemned to a stiller doom than mine, and millions are in silent revolt against their lot.

CHARLOTTE BRONTË

At first the Bishop asked her for the truth,
that blandly Latin script that ploughed his tongue,
but each new symbol, sound to fit the glyphs,
would contradict his righteous alphabet
and so he found a clue in singeing flesh:
her drowning, hanging footless from the pine.

And yet her words would fly to him as birds,
years later when the speaker was long dead:
often the hummingbird's red-throated whir;
the vulture's prod for jelly, beak for eyes;
stern eagles swooping on his Indian fig,
while nets retrieved the mystery of cranes.

How could he know tenors of stony glyphs,
their mathematics of an ageing sky.
He sensed a toothless woman in the moon,
but missed the honey harvest of the fly.
He never saw a crone shoulder the sun,
nor knew the lighthouse of the northern star.

The tally of misreading soon advanced
so legions of proud glyphs were rapt by flames,
but speaking in the ballast-base of clay,
new villages were made from wet leaf-beds,
where souls escape to buzz about the pines
and ripening flowers are budding to be read.

Catskin

To break the man's advance, she asks for a dress of spun silver
and he breaks open stone for a metallic clasp.

To evade the miner's reach, she calls for a coat of beaten gold
and he digs fathoms to leaf her body.

To stop the hunter's mouth, she begs for all the feathers
of all the birds on earth, which he skins for their riches.

Only in her catskin, he cannot find her
and, in it, she escapes with many coats.

Later and later, she finds her desire and salves
herself with silver by the shining puddle.

She lines herself with gold and draws you to the kitchen,
the saucepans stacked by the broken ladle.

With feathers limed, she flies to you: the maid
that skims each morning's milk for cream.

Under the dawn, you change your pelts to catskin,
rippling your backs in a growl of pleasure.

Returning with his mallet, knife and chisel, the man
finds only two cats shaking their ears in the rain.

My Spinalonga Passion

Desires lost for the lack of trying,
haunt the frightened trees on Spinalonga,
sing a wind that cripples cypress branches.

Each day, the tourists ride out on boats
to Spinalonga Island; they stand on a squint
of sand and, beyond the jetty, snaked spray
shivers, stings their faces. They retreat to land:
glass cases in the once-darkened houses of lepers.
Here a Byzantine bronze lion, his tail making
a figure of eight and there, a bow
of the Ottoman Empire missing an arrow.

Paths all over Spinalonga are walked smooth:
the circle that rounds the island's hump
where lepers dreamed of detonating
Turkish battlements. Paths extend
from hospital door to hospice gate:
the boulderous top where a church became
a mosque that opened a grave in Venetian alleys,
and fathoms of blackened hospital windows.

Here I wait for you, swathed in milky bandages.
Frail as a reflection, I offer one receding hand
and the whole of my beautiful, infected body.

Atlas-eating

The atlas-eater with a jaw for news,
Bit out the mandrake with tomorrow's scream.

DYLAN THOMAS, 'Altarwise by Owl-Light'

In atlas charts and longitudes, in plots
and plans and latitudes, the new found land
gives up its lard for the fattening
of Spanish cathedrals, its gridded gold
wired into archives of cartography,
where tomes of maps are mercantile bondsmen
and the only sound that matters on earth
is the rat-a-tat-tat of a coin on teeth.
At home, blueprints are filed in marbled office cells
by clerks who regard Columbus' script
but never tremble. The maps of harbours,
with their sea snakes and turtles, are nothing
compared to creatures gathered onshore:
the squat, warted toad of the colony.

Grudges grow deep in new-coming colonists:
mandragora buried in a graveyard plot,
watered with semen and honey to shore up
the slime and decay of their outpost land.
They slow-bake their greed until it is nothing
but ashes in their fires; they feel it fatten
under shirts and doublets, still harbouring
toothsome grudges. The mandrake's syrupy gold,
and the lust on their faces is an age-old script:
starving on the shore of a new geography.
Out of the alchemy of colony cells,
white and tubercular grow the New World men.
Parasitic, they swell from soil to burst:
and shriek like mandrakes torn out of the earth.

The Mandrake Baby

I've read that if you bury a mandrake in earth,
water it daily and leave it to ant colonies,
it grows a baby's face, the soft mouth
of a child or a foetus in its garden plot.
Today, at the hospital, I heard an old woman
tell this tale, my grandmother's voice from the shore
of a far country. I heard it in the clinic cell
when my baby died like a whale onland
in the dull, persistent light of the sonograph.
Why the baby was lost: I would give anything
to know, but the American doctor has a script
of platitudes: mandrake flowers, inflated and fat.
My baby still waxes onscreen, lunar and golden,
a tiny moon in my womb too barren to be born.

Like Tamzene Donner did

Like Tamzene Donner did, the newlyweds bear their
losses over mountains, and run to earth on tarmac needled
with spiny pine, paved in gold of alder leaves. Here, the
grudge of the colony (that despises newcomers) is enough
to fatten and tip them to vertigo. The unfurling tongues
of cornfields go by, rigid as a teleprompter's script, while
a scarecrow points to Route 80, plotted in deserts of salt.
They dump some of their things from the trunk – his
books, her mother's ottoman on the road. By the car, he
signs an autograph in the dust with a stick; she draws the
shoreline of California, the mouse ears of Disneyland.
More likely, they'll find themselves in a sheriff's cell.

Stopping past Donner Lake, a gas station sells warm cans
of coke and an old man's tale bears out what Tamzene
Donner did: *He died on scrubland – her husband sheltering
from blizzards; his time on earth was done, though she carried
him on just to be sure, then hurried away. In the snow, his
hair was gold with the sunrise, but she had to leave without
map or graph of the Rockies, struggling through snow to the
colony, over Hastings' Cut-Off without guide or kinsman.* At
the end, their car stalls in fattening snow and mountains
peaks turn: their hungering faces closing while he burns.
By his cemetery plot, she'll put on his suit: she's willing
to go, but has no script.

Farming Florida

The Lunar Sea Motel is not like its description
in the 50s guide book: the room is a cell
for cockroaches and the garden lot is a tarmac plot.
The long peninsula is a shallow shelf, which bears
the concrete sprawl, rimmed by the sea's two lips.
On a 1953 map of Florida's high and low lands,
fruit, truck, peanuts and hogs – everything
that sells – is labelled on the limestone earth.
A small-printed footnote tells of a rare flower, fattened
from 500 years' growth and miles inland from shore.
In the everglade heart – unknown to homestead men –
companioned by bears, panthers and the golden eyes
of alligators, the Giant Orchid colonises
the swamp, deep-rooted in its leeching geography.

Love and the Orchid

Like a strange exotic plant, love grows in arid soil.
ROSEMARY SULLIVAN, *Labyrinth of Desire*

Most of us will only ever see photographs
of the Ghost Orchid, or maybe hear descriptions
of its papery bracts, the invisible root colony
that lifts the ghost flower up in the dank cells
of the swamp. The Giant Sphinx Moth gilds
its proboscis tongue in delicious orchid plots:
the blossoms – each as big as the hand of a man.
Sometimes love appears like this: a pale face borne
up by sadness through the trees, a moon over the shore
or a percussive knowledge that opens like a mouth.
Who knows what desires are blooming, fattening
in the depths of the woods? Our bleak dreamlands
open to mine shafts or passages under the earth:
never-ending and hardly ever leading to anything.

Grown out of barren spaces, dark knots, the things
we try to ignore, there flowers a slow choreography
of longing. We lift our faces from the limestone earth:
the white orchid petals that beg for inscription
by moth tongues. Or we are the insects that land
on every bright flower we can colonise,
never sure if this one is richest, the fattest.
We cross the ocean like the orchid seed-cells
that blew over the Atlantic in the keening mouth
of the wind; we drink at every cup of gold
that we can find, sink our roots into every shore.
In the glade, I wait in my very own plot,
my roots tracked and torn, and still I bear
the orchids yearning like men, like women.

Pennsylvania Winter

The blizzard falls over us with muzzling silence, though workmen
scrape with plastic shovels, and in the stripped tree, something
is rasping: tiny teeth grating on a nut. Even the bears
are sleeping, not even the hot stench of animal shit to autograph
the snow. The leaves, too, are deep for wading in forest plots;
they never die but stay to bloody the snow and loamy earth.
The territory drifts beside the water, along the shoreline
of Lake Erie; its crust of ice is thick enough to carry conscripts.
Soldiers new-minted, embroidered with green and gold,
skirmish on the whitened beach hoping for garlands.
I walk home through the forest, where holes in the earth open
with fear, with desire: an underground maze of colonies.
Something is growing, blossoming with frost in every cell:
the snow drifts up to the window now and is still fattening.

All of which are American dreams

American dreams are ill-fitting shoes that fatten
your heel to a blister. They appear as a figure
that you try to greet from a long way off; to your call,
lost in the din of the city, he never answers anything.
There are long cherished dreams that we colonise:
dreams are feathery seed pods which are borne
on the wind to catch on our sleeves, in sterile hair;
dreams are hands inked by grimy photographs
or newsprint; dreams are blazing: the land-burning
of forest fires that blacken burnished harvest plots;
dreams are flies that buzz and glint their wings gold;
they are dull vibrations entering your body through earth,
or they are a tinny song, the mumblings of a radio script
heard underwater, or from the breeze on a distant shore.

American dreams are whirring at night to shore us up
against doubt: the fears that are always fattening.
Like Fay Wray who screamed her way out of the script
of *King Kong*, dreams are shrieking: a mother bereft.
Or they silently worm their way in the tunnelled earth,
wheedling openings from the bars of every prison cell.
Their dreams infect you like the fever for gold,
though you know they'll never amount to anything.
But above all these dreams cultivate love, their plots
small among the multitude longings of the colony,
where we yearn for men or women of our dreamlands:
the passages and shafts of sleep where desire is born.
And all the lovers burning in the New World geography
dream, like you and me, of one slow, inevitable touch.

Arches

From the flat-floored desert rolled low by heat, hungering and gold,
to the high-stacked desert, wave-formed in ridged bodies.

We fill ourselves with gaps, gorges, passageways: the stubborn things
of the desert. We follow canyon walls that were once the shore
of a million-year-ago sea: Lake Boneville dissolving cell
by cell.
   We learn stone layers of lava and sand, the geography
of Utah rivers: the Dirty Devil, Virgin and San Juan plotting
their desires through salted rock.
        Beneath the junipers and fat
pinions, we drowse on beds of sagebrush, yellow needles and earth.

All through this narrow country, the sickling arches hang and bear
the emptiness, eons of stone from before a colony
occupied bleak expanses with evidences and scripture.

The archways erode to a long cry, while the *Mayflower* men
build their settlement: a rancid poultice that infects the land.

The Heart of the Sorrowing Coyote

Crossing the Rockies, blending with the land,
Coyote steals her way in furs of cream; the gold
of her pelt is almost invisible to the cattlemen:
the sac full of pups in her rawboned body.
At evening, we hear her bellowing a script
of howls, which startles the pithy, yielding things
in the night, and alarms the seething colonies:
those dull pioneers hatching on the lakeshore.
Her bellyful of whelps is ready to be born
in the coiling bowl of a stony cratered cell,
while the moon sucks at the earth's gravity
and fireflies circulate like points in a star graph.
Even while she births them, their deaths are fattening,
and the men in the valley scour out new plots.

Infertility

Doctors have their ways to investigate: microscope eyes
that count the glittering fish of sperm, cameras that stalk
beaded eyes into the gorgeous-red heart of the cervix.
The ultrasound wand probes, presses, sucks to measure the orb
of each egg in its sac, while x-rays unravel the womb,
a stretched concertina that spasms even as it fills
with saline. Later there's chemical mingling of your blood
and mine, to map how XY arms and legs of chromosomes
embrace or fist. Here I am in the stark, unforgiving
sonographer's light: a passage, narrow key, squat cave
gorged by blood, or just a ripening plum with arid seeds.
Here am I, a woman not a body, in the snowlight
outside the hospital, where I smear the whitened sidewalk
and run with my long legs, my pretty body still unveined,
still to be spoiled by the loving-soft fat of motherhood.
So many women come to me saying, 'I have lost too,
and this one, and this one.' So many embryos retreat
to flesh: the live cell of the mother. Don't tell me that it
will happen for me, when the only sure thing is a miracle:
the sperm nuzzling in its nest and the egg that opens, explodes.

The Guide

On Wednesday, I caught a bus to the Sierra Norte. You need a guide up there, because the forests are fierce and you can easily lose your way. The locals rent out cabins and offer their services as guides. Eustorgio, was a cheerful man, and extremely patient. He showed me the flowers and plants of the mountains: Rosa de la Montaña – the red thistle, mushrooms good to eat, and leaves that curbed toothaches.

When we reached a crossroads between the hard and easy routes, Eustorgio advised me to take the easy path. Of course I chose the difficult way, and Eustorgio led me upwards. I took off my glove and he held my hand in places where we needed to climb. It was the season when no wind blows through the cloud-forests. The path climbed steadily along the Devil's Backbone. Eustorgio told me: 'Look ahead – not sideways, not behind.' Every so often, a cloud passed over and plunged us into mist.

Late in the afternoon, we came to a cabin. Eustorgio told me it belonged to his uncle. He was scattering food on the waters of the fishponds.

– 'It's pretty', I said.
– 'My uncle built it for his wife,' he explained, 'But she could not live with him. That's how it is with you isn't it?'
– 'I don't know what you mean,' I said.

Back in town, I ate chicken stew at the comedor. Eustorgio led me back to the hostel and built a fire. He painfully copied my e-mail address in a small diary. He said he wouldn't be there in the morning, because he was driving to the city. I sat by the fire and waited. We sat in silence for a while and, at last, he left.

The Angel and the Subway

On the threshold between everything under the earth
and the bean-hill colony of NYC, a northbound train
bears my love to Houston Street, carries a kiss
with every silvered carriage cell. The New York subway
and Chicago L-train, the Washington Metro
and Boston T only serve to remind me
of how little I know my own London Underground
though I've dreamed of its passages, my desire
spiralling like stairwells, spinning like whirligigs;
it radiates from me as heat, as radio waves.

Under the gaze of the Underground passengers,
bodies pressed together like packed market fruit,
I am no longer a 'reasonably attractive woman'
but a crippled girl twisting like newspaper.
And over the hive of the London subway station,
Piccadilly Circus beams out brands onscreen
while imperial theatres gleam luminous as bone.
That statue of an archer on Shaftesbury Fountain:
they call it 'Eros', or the Angel of Charity,
though really it's 'Anteros', love requited or avenged.

And when I am away from you, travelling
by tube, streetcar or trolley, in subterranean passages
of American cities, I bring to mind the most subtle
signs of love I can recall: your fingers in my hair;
awkward leaning on your arm while your eyes
unspindle me without saying a word.
Deep in the inky tube windows, a pale thumbprint
of a question quavers, judders as the carriage halts:
why I never recognise those who love me, always
mistaking *anteros* for *eros*, selfless for selfish love?

The Love of a Husband

Because when she shuts a door, he opens a window.

Because he knows the traps of timetables, schedules.

Because he comes home with punnets of wet, ripe strawberries.

Because he stretches his arms and legs like a cat.

Because he climbed the Cairn of Wrath at Whitesands Beach.

Because he smells of chalk and wet grass.

Because he cured her fear of heights by leading her up Mayan temples.

Because his fingers are calloused from pressing strings on the double bass.

Because he thought she was Joan of Arc.

Because, buying her ring in a New York store, he knew the right size
       without asking.

Because he cycles to work every morning, even in the drifting snow.

Because he is afraid of dogs, especially small ones.

Because sometimes at night, his hand reaches out for her.

Because his vision is 20/10.

Because he waits for her to come to him.

Because he walks through the untidy house without noticing.

Because his beard scratches her cheek.

Because he said, if she was Marx, he was Engels pulling her back to earth.

Because he never cries at films, but she does.

Because he works in pure, not applied, mathematics.

Because he never refuses a meal of any description.

Because he looked up the words of a Neruda poem: t*u cuerpo alegre, tus
       luminosos ojos.*

Because he means everything he says.

Because he knows the shape of her and how she likes to be touched.

Because he never, ever hesitated.

Because when she shuts a window, he opens a door.

The Blue Rose

(i.m. James Earnest Brigley)

His roses grew in my grandmother's flowerbeds,
in the garden where the pale green gate fitted the latch.
The word, *rose*, as well travelled as he was:
rosa the Latin made from the Greek *rhodea*
from Aramaic *wurdda* that mimics Iranian *warda*.
Late in his garden, blooms that bowed to his stoop
now pay him remembrance; the fine Floribunda
Miniature Cupcake and hardy Polyantha.

Not Nyasaland figs or the Belizean black orchid,
but the Impressionist, Comanche and Montezuma;
the twiggy Green Rose and Crested Sweetheart
as staunch in their thanks as the Stanwell Perpetual;
the purpled, speckled Song of the Stars; the Alba rose
wet in the dew and the furious heads of American Pillars;
the Othello rose nesting woe in its folds
and the gilded blossoms of the Climbing Peace.

In the late silence of his rooms without gardens,
did he shrink in grief to a tiny Tom Thumb?
Or did he lift the latch on the pale green gate to find
a riot of thorns, a wilderness of bourbons, as sweet
and pungent as a dose of dopamine to the brain?
Only the ripening blue rose of forgetfulness,
tended by his care, grows beyond remembering.
as full as a moon and still in bloom.

THE LADY AND THE UNICORN

After the tapestries at the Musée de Cluny, Paris

It fell upon a little western flower,
Before milk-white, now purple with love's wound

WILLIAM SHAKESPEARE

Prologue

It begins in my grandmother's garden
with Bristol roses that blossom all year.
The barbered lawn that is mowed each day
borders the soil-beds of riotous plants:
eglantine blossoms are apple on the tongue;
sprigged stalks of medicinal thyme;
oxlips speckled yellow; and suckling flowers
of strangling woodbine, edible and sweet.
Beyond the garden gate, carbon-black wreckage
of a police-bike smoulders, burnt out.
We hear the splintering of a bottle or window:
an angry mob beats on the garden walls.

I Behind Orchard Walls

A fully grown woman, I find high walls
and cloister myself as a nunning gardener.
Early I wake to attack the wreckage
of brambling berries, holly under my window.
My tumbled Paris orchard is richly planted
with oak, pine and orange trees that flower
to pendulous fruit; I brew them yearly
to orange-water tea or rich marmalade.
The ancient orchard sees out today
and tomorrow, while the city outside
unwinds long cement arms, and at night-time,
it swallows the moon with its luminous mouth.

II The Myth of the Unicorn

I know him to be a unicorn by his spiralling eye,
though he walks in the shape of a man in these walls.
For him to catalogue the orchard will take some time,
the perennials grown before the plantations;
before voyages by sea; before the *Mayflower*
crossed the Atlantic to make a garden
of America; before the golden continents of years
colonised the best, the brightest of the day.
I have read that the unicorn's horn spirals out
like the tusk of the narwhal that wrecks
the hopes of passing sailboats. The narrow window
of chance always seems the sweetest.

III Tasting the Garden

In the cottage kitchen, tarts and sweetcakes
crumble; dough rolls out in long tongues.
I am up to my elbows in sugar and flour,
and the gas oven's moan passes the time.
I shut out poor creatures from the tomato-plants,
red orbs of the glasshouse, and beyond the walls,
stray dogs in their hunger salivate and sniff them out.
On the sill, a plastic dish of seed speeds this year's
journey of swifts, a nightingale that hides most days.
Dressed in finch's gold, I look to the window
but it reflects back only the darkening garden:
the honey of all my appetites wrecked.

IV The Face in the Mirror

Because all my faith in pleasure is wrecked,
not even the unicorn's visits are sweet.
I find I mistrust my caller at times,
when he pulls on his boots and coat to go out
into the orchard, as if before the year
is out, he'll be a fox to ravage my garden.
Or just a man in a horse's head, garlanded flowers
hung about him: each one a falsehood planted?
As I feed the birds, so he gives morsels each day
to a woman like me, bricked up and walled
by the very first desire that sat on my tongue
and the pain that shattered me to an empty window.

When I close a door to him, he finds a window
and what does it matter: one more break-in, another wreck
of a promise? I have been his mirror all this time
and he gazes into me as if to find himself out.
He is smaller in the glass though his legs are planted
as if in readiness for some disaster: the collapse of years.
The spell of his eye breaks when his ego flowers
to nothing, so he is only a man in the garden.
No matter what he does outside these walls,
what taxis caught, reports written, what sweetnesses
he hopes to find rolling across his tongue,
he cannot stop gazing for the rest of the day.

V Walls Have Ears

I venture out down Rue d'École on a wet Sunday,
the pavements slick with light from shop windows.
In a record store, I buy an LP of *Où Vont Les Fleurs?*
sung by Dietrich; that voice of hers, heavy and sweet.
Spun on the antique Victrola, her song climbs the walls
of the orchard, a long sigh from the garden.
Just as I prune magnolia to the espalier each year,
so I teach myself to face the shocks and jolts outside:
brash horns, the bang of the Métro, rapid tongues
of late nightclubs, footsteps scattered and mistimed.
I train to the trellis what once was wrecked,
and await the springtime of candling plants.

VI Full Moon, Full Bloom

One slow summer, years ago, the electricity plant
collapsed to blackness at the wane of day
and I sat with a battery torch while the sun wrecked
itself on the far hills and plunged into night-time.
Just like then, the spiral of my unicorn's eye
taunts me that this sudden blaze will blow out,
and leave me chained again in the garden,
collared under the oaks and the trellis that flowers
silently, darkly in the prison of these walls.
All night, he is a flaming victory flag, a lit window
in the dark, where nothing can disturb the sweetness
of my long-ago dreams, the desire of my budding years.

VII Don't Touch

Under the narrow bed of my student years,
I kept a French Marigold, its roots replanted
in a pot. Some say its smell which sits on the tongue
is unpleasant, but never to the lonely gardener
who learns her slow trade day by day,
hoping for more than a season's sweetness.
I remember a shop that sells marigold seeds
near Rue du Temple, and walk with an eye out
for its bright window. But today there's a wreck:
the car at the busy intersection, its windows
smashed, a van's bonnet buckled against a wall,
and a man on the corner passing time.

He just stands and stares the whole time;
the tram's bell clangs as it does year in, year out,
and I wait there beside him watching the wrecked
passengers, bloodied and dazed in the daylight.
When he brushes past, his hands are unsweetened
by the love I am used to in gardens,
where in their solitude, the blossoms that flower
are only found by the bee's curling tongue.
And I think now how women have always been outed,
broken, dissected, grafted, transplanted.
I pay for the seeds that bless the shop-window,
and turn for my home, my crumbling orchard walls.

VIII The Lantern, Dog and Thorn

Now when I'm alone, the great stone walls
are a closed fist blocking my exit. How many times
has the unicorn asked me to sweeten
our meetings with boat rides, walks at Jardin des Plantes,
or shopping in the dusk of shortening days?
With his catalogue finished, my tongue
is syrupy, caked in my mouth, words wrecked
by what I cannot say, what I do not spell out.
I find myself alone at the end of the year,
the moon a smoking lamp above my garden,
dogs growling, and under my window,
honeyed and wax tapers in their final flowering.

IX À mon seul désir

It's open now on weekday afternoons: the flowerbeds
tidy and taut, trailing plants espaliered to the walls.
A laminated flyer tells the opening times,
but I visit at the end of a summer weekday.
In the dusk, I use the key kept for the wreck
of a cottage with gas stove and rattling windows.
Though never a very good gardener, the sweetness
of night magnolia musk is all of my own planting.
But still, the old command of previous years
is spelled by the toll of city bells. *Do not dare to go out
of these woods.* The chimes knell over the garden
pealing midnight dreams with their iron tongues.

Lady, Lion, Unicorn

Under my window, with a feigning tongue,
a lion or unicorn sings in the garden, demanding years
of laddered days, longing for stretched seasons of time.
Whichever he is, he refuses to go out of these walls: out
of lawn-dew and sickly-sweet nectar, out of the wreckage
of holly-barbs, globular flowers and stalks of pieplants.

Barbed holly, globed flowers and stalking pieplants,
dewy lawns and sweet-sick nectar all grown from a wreck.
Out of these walls, he cannot go. Whatever he is, he's out
of season, the long days laddered and stretched for time.
Lion and unicorn demand the song of my garden years:
my tongue under figs, gown in the wind.

*   *   *

Home from Home

'Why did you leave Wales to go to this barren country?'

Letter from the Welsh shoemaker, John Gordon Jones,
to preacher, Iorthryn Gwynedd of Pennsylvania,
dated December 30th 1851

Highway after roadway after freeway after carriageway, a
ladder of film flickers by the passenger window.

She is not the surprise of Lake Erie's swallowing mouth, but
the long stripes of terraces on a bleak mountain. She is never
the twigs crackling in perpetual forests, or the milky crust of
frozen rivers, but she is the flowerbed of Mr Lloyd. where
she picked his bloom in despair.

The last time she went home, the town was waiting, as
though someone had told it she was coming back. Do you
love me? said the river. What shall we call our children?
asked the churned turf of the Llynfi Road pitch. You'll never
be beautiful: the wind in the trees over Llangynwyd Ceme-
tery. Where have you been hiding? barking dogs straining
their leashes.

She is not the candied cream bone of a possum skull, or any
other dead things in American forests. But she is the crow in
crown: a prince named Bran circled by castles. She is not the
Chinook winds whistling hot about the ears and eyes, but
she is the Pembrokeshire grafting of pear and apple trees.

She is the Dau Gleddau, two rivers that split to swords, and
she is a woman on deck, travelling alone across the Irish Sea.
She is a puddler feeding the pot-bellied ironworks, the dizzy-
ing shaft of the coal mine, and long nails hammered in Cardiff
Docks.

There it is again: the heartwrench of the road, both carrying
her away and taking her home.

NOTES

My Last Rochester was written during a residency at the Brontë Parsonage Museum in Haworth, Yorkshire. During the residency, I had access to objects in the museum archives such as the hair bracelet and the perfume bottle. I draw on Juliet Barker's *The Brontës*, *The Brontë Myth* by Lucasta Miller, *Selected Letters of Charlotte Brontë* edited by Margaret Smith, 'Charlotte Brontë's Letters to M. Heger' by Linda S. Kauffman and Mary Jacobus's essay 'The Buried Letter'.

The bishop in **Glyph** (32) is Bishop Diego de Landa who lived in the Mexican Yucatán during the sixteenth century.

Spinalonga Island in **My Spinalonga Passion** (34) is a real place off the coast of Crete, which was occupied by the Venetians and by the Ottoman Empire. It was a leper colony from 1903 to 1957.

Tamzene Donner (37) was a member of the Donner Party which set out for California in 1846. At the 'Hastings Cut-Off', the group was stranded, snowbound and reduced to cannibalism.

The title of **All of which are American dreams** (41) is a reference to the Rage Against the Machine song, 'Know Your Enemy'.

Arches (42) is a 'cut-up' poem which is made of words from an article on Utah in *The School and Library Atlas of the World* (1979) and from a piece on Arches National Park in *National Geographic's Guide to the National Parks of the United States* (2009).

The Blue Rose (48) is dedicated to my English grandfather, James Earnest Brigley.

The Lady and the Unicorn (49) was written after the tapestries of the same name at the Musée National de Moyen Age (Musée de Cluny), Paris. There are six tapestries in all, with five representing the senses, and the last one titled *À mon seul désir*. You can view them on the museum website: http://www.musee-moyenage.fr/ang/.

'The Lady and the Unicorn' uses a variation on the double sestina form, as do poems in the sequence titled 'Conquest' from 'Atlas-eating' to 'Heart of the Sorrowing Coyote'.

The epigraph to **Home from Home** (61) is an extract from a letter which appears in a translation of *America, or a Variety of Notes on the United States of Interest to Immigrants* by Iorthryn Gwynedd (found in Swansea University Library). The place names in the poem are all from the Llynfi Valley in South Wales.

ACKNOWLEDGEMENTS

A poem from this collection received the English Association's Poetry Fellows' Award and another was shortlisted in the Arvon International Poetry Competition. Poems from this collection have been published in the *Arvon International Poetry Competition Anthology 2010*, *Agenda* (the Welsh special issue, and John Burnside special issue), *Best American Poetry Blog* (feature on young British poets), *Blossombones*, the Worple anthology *Dove Release, Gists and Piths, Horizon, Like Starlings, Lung Jazz: Young British Poets for Oxfam, Maintenant 5: A Contemporary Dada Poetry Journal, Poetry Ireland Review, Poetry Salzburg, Poetry Wales, Polarity, Roundyhouse, Southword, The Manhattan Review* (feature on young British poets), *The Lampeter Review, The Platte Valley Review* and *The New Welsh Review*.

Thanks to the following organisations: the Arvon Foundation, the Brontë Parsonage Museum, the English Association, Literature Wales, Marlborough College, Northampton University, the Nittany Valley Writers' Network, the National Association of Writers in Education, Otto Books, Shakespeare and Co. (Paris), Webster's Books, and Yr Academi Gymreig/The Welsh Academy.

Thanks to the following people who have supported and inspired me in different ways – mentors, editors and friends: James Adler, Sonya Andermahr, Meredith Andreas, Charles and Phillippa Bennett, Peter Blegvad, Julie Boden, Colin Brown, Peter Carlaftes, Peter Carpenter, Elisha Clark Halpin, Helen Dennis, Jane Dowson, Carrie Etter, Simon Fletcher, Chloe Garner, Kat Georges, Mike Golby, Wolfgang Görtschacher, Kathryn Gray, Greg Halpin, David Hart, A.A. Hedge Coke, Jane Holland, Jenna Holmes, Ros Hudis, Hilary Jenkins, Caleb Klaces, Caitríona O'Reilly, Leanne O'Sullivan, Rob A. Mackenzie, Robert Minhinnick, Lisa Mooney Smith, Paul Munden, Lawrence Phillips, Mike Ponsford, Chris Ringrose, Zoë Skoulding, Susan Slaviero, Virginia Tate Meadows, Alexandra Trowbridge-Matthews, Sue Williams, and Janet Wilson. Thanks too for generous, rigorous attention of those readers who helped me redraft this manuscript: Andy Brown, Richard Chamberlain, Amy Evans, David Morley, Pascale Petit, Patricia McCarthy, Erika L. Sanchez, and Todd Swift.

Special thanks to Victoria Brookland for her artwork.

Thanks most of all to my husband Dan Thompson for his enduring patience and unconditional love.